RISING **AT 5 AM**

Other Books by Marc Elihu Hofstadter:

House of Peace (Mother's Hen Press)
Visions (Scarlet Tanager Press)
Shark's Tooth (Regent Press)
Luck (Scarlet Tanager Press)

For Jannie,

With love,

Marc

RISING AT 5 AM

Poetry by

Marc Elihu Hofstadter

Latitude Press
Pittsburg, California

These poems have appeared in the following magazines:
Berkeley Poetry Review: “Winging It with Kenneth Koch”
RiverSedge: “Every Night,” “Spring”
Tea: “On Not Reading *Walden*”
These poems have appeared in the anthology, *My Dreaming Waking Life*: “Rainbow,” “A Little Night Music,” “What Love Tells Me”

Printed in the United States of America

Cover image: color printed etching with hand-drawn additions in ink and watercolor, “Albion Rose, or Glad Day, or The Dance of Albion” by William Blake, ca. 1794, copyright © The Trustees of the British Museum, London, U.K.

Library of Congress Control Number: 2009939609
ISBN 978-0-9819534-0-3

Published by
Latitude Press, imprint of RAW ArT PRESS
www.rawartpress.com
Trena Machado, Publisher

Cover Design: Inez Machado
Author Photo: Mayona Engdahl

for David Zurlin

Acknowledgments

Like most things in life, a book isn't the product of an imagination working in isolation, it's in some sense a joint effort created by a community of people. Some of those who have played a part in the generation of this volume are: Joe Chaiklin, Leonard J. Cirino, Jannie Dresser, Patricia Edith, Dian Gillmar, Gloria Grover, Dave Holt, Dale Jensen, Stephen Kessler, Jeanne Lupton, Clive Matson, Florence Miller, Janell Moon, David Mus, Sunny Solomon, Elaine Starkman, Jan Steckel and Judy Wells. A major share of whatever in the book is good has been contributed by my dedicated publisher and editor, Trena Machado, who has pored over the manuscript with her expert writer's eye in addition to dealing with all the vicissitudes of the publication process. Most of all, though, it's my partner David Zurlin who has made the book possible, for he has shared my days and thoughts with constant care, dedication and love.

CONTENTS

RAINBOW

UTTER LOVE

JOHN SINGER SARGENT'S MALE NUDES

HEROES

DAYS AND YEARS

RAINBOW

Rainbow

I picked it apart with my prism,
separating red from orange,
orange from yellow,
yellow from gold,
each color individual, pure.
I thought of myself
as an adventurer of color.
Then I napped, and in my dream
red people cried because
they'd never known an orange person,
orange people wanted to be yellow,
yellow people were stuck forever
in yellowness. I awoke
and looked out the window
wishing to see the old,
multicolored myth,
the one with a pot at its end,
but there was only blue sky.

Old Baudelaire

after the first line of Adam Zagajewski's poem "Old Marx (2)"
as translated by Clare Cavanagh

I try to envision his last winter,
the ceiling sloping sharply,
the window leaking in the cold.
His throat, his groin, hurt.
He felt older than his years.
The absinthe warmed his belly.
He wondered if he'd done things right.
If his words were anything more
than self-indulgence.
He was alone, his beauties
having slipped away
into the black Parisian night.
Then he remembered
one of his own lines, *Hear, my dear,*
hear sweet night approach,
and he smiled, a smile
that slowly broadened
to take in the room,
the city,
then the world.

Scattered

A Marxist and a Pointillist,
I played lacrosse, slept in sight of
the spires of San Francisco
and the night sky over Provence,
grinning with Van Gogh stars.

Tattooed, pierced punks own a chunk of me.
Disciplined twelve-tone composers, too.

I play a tough third base,
feel at home with drag queens.

Some of me goes—God forgive!—
with literary critics,
another glides along the chrome bars
of gleaming ballet studios.

I left a bit of myself in Orléans
with its wedding cake cathedral.
A portion still swims
in Jerusalem's golden light.

Cruised for men in the Castro,
escorted a rich, snobbish girl
to a ritzy high school prom.

Asleep, the deepest mystery of myself.
Not sure who I am—
a creature who hardly knows his name,
a wraith who's sought firm ground
but gotten lost in the maze of time.

The Mime

in memory of Marcel Marceau

He spoke in silence.
His words were a hat, a leaf, a smile.
He lifted us up with two gloved hands
and played with us a while.
What he did in his other life,
what kind of voice
he had, I don't know.
Only this mattered:
how he made us feel,
how we loved him.

Cat on a Piano

The cat tinkles the piano keys by stepping
gingerly, each paw sounding a black or
white note. So by simply acting in the
world we make a music we do not intend
that reverberates throughout the house.

Street Artist

for Marvin Sanders

The shabby street filled with scales and arpeggios
that flew from your lips:
sylvan Debussy, florid Bach, vivid Vivaldi.
Your red plaid shirt was holey,
your jeans soiled rags.
I dropped a dollar in the upturned beret on the sidewalk
and we talked.
You were without ambition,
content merely to play and live.
Play and live!
What was I doing trying to win prizes
when art is to be loved wholly for its own sake?
Marvin, I won't forget your lesson:
write not for designer shirts or book contracts
but for silvery flashes of words on water
like the rippling runs of your fluttering flute.

On Not Reading *Walden*

In this small-town, country coffeehouse
the man at the next table is reading *Walden*.
I've read it three times and cherish it.
I envy him a little.
But my Lapsang Souchong tea tastes smoky
and the breeze is swaying the blossoming pear tree
so I sit back and breathe deep the scent of pear,
and reflect that sometimes it's good not to read.

Swelled Head

Am I the whole world?
When I fall asleep, the earth seems
to disappear like a damsel
in a magician's box.
Awake, I can't hear anyone
else's thoughts, just my own
throbbing, throbbing.
I'm not self-centered but,
try as I may, I can't
wiggle anyone else's toes.
Yet they say solipsism's bad—
I can't help the poor
if I don't admit they exist.
What do you say, reader?
Aren't you, too, the only one home?

In Common

That guy in stained rags sipping
coffee at the next table could be
me so easily, just some brief
switch of energies and *poof*!
I'd be him muttering to himself,
stuck in his identity like fruit
in a can, unable to escape
except through words or death,
those two liberators, and I think
of trying to speak to him but I don't
because he's suffering and I'm not.
Yet I'll see him on the other shore.

I, Icarus

I'd like to figure it all out before I die,
like my father who wanted to know everything.
Then death wouldn't be as scary, I think,
but terror chills my chest as I attain the heights,
the wings he gave me melt, I plunge
into the surging swells where I thrash and struggle
just like him.

Small

Small am I amidst galaxies
spinning and swirling, black holes
sucking planets in, supernovae blasting
light and matter to kingdom come, dark
energy enigmatically driving worlds
apart—what can I do except
live a little better every day?

Whaaa...?

Why do we have ten toes
instead of eight?
Why are planets spheres,
not squares?
Why does love
feel so good?
I don't get
what makes a man handsome,
why the world's
divided into countries,
why there's so much space
between the stars.
Maybe you can explain
some of these things,
but there's one question
I'm pretty sure
you can't answer,
whether you're physicist,
philosopher or poet:
why all is here in the first place.

Riddle

I've never been to Cuba,
never touched the Rio Grande,
never kissed a girl I loved,
never lent a friendly hand.
I'm an old doctor,
a true farmer,
a stagecoach driver,
a two-timer.
May I receive full commission,
discover my vocation,
be granted a full pardon,
ride home a winner.

Tired of Tea

I haven't drunk a cup in five weeks.
One hundred and two tins, all different,
sit forlorn on my shelf.
Instead, I down orange juice.
None of my friends know yet.
Keemun and Nilgiri
don't do it for me anymore.
Things end, but I never thought
it'd come to this.
Now, I savor each sip of Coke,
wondering how long it will last.

Red Balloon

I waded through a tepid morning conference,
wolfed down a burger and fries,
waited an hour to get my blood drawn,
got routine news from my doctor at 3:00,
then struggled home in the evening commute.
Yet I was able, between the blood draw
and the doctor, to squeeze in forty minutes
in a coffeehouse sipping Persian tea
and savoring a doughy bagel.
Isn't it like that? We grab happiness
out of the wind, then let it go like a balloon,
bright red, that advertises its joy,
then hemorrhages air as it spins away
into the vast sky.

Staying Up Late

I like to stay awake after
everyone else is asleep.
In the stillness I thrill to
Dickinson's solitude,
bathe in Chopin's lonely pride,
watch CNN as though
the last witness on earth.
At 2:00 A.M., I pick up steam
and write my poems.
By 3:00, I'm sailing along,
a sloop on open waters.
I feel I could live forever.
At 5:00, I put skull to pillow
to soak in the news on radio.
At 6:00, I still want
the night to last.

UTTER LOVE

Every Night

in memory of Constantine Cavafy

Every night he goes to the city
to find a man to sleep with.
Each time he meets a different one,
kisses wet-tongued mouths,
strokes satin shoulders,
thighs strong as elm limbs,
hair-studded bellies.
He's never satisfied.
Each night he dreams of a youth,
hair like wheat in the sun,
eyes flat Sierra lakes,
who sees through him, all of him.
As the two embrace,
a circle of light locks them together.
Every night he searches.
But in his dream, and nowhere else,
does he find such utter love.

The Razor

I'd go to Mario's for haircuts
in New York City when I was eight,
intrigued by the swirling red-and-white
pole and by his dark wrists with their
jet black hair. The high point
was when he'd lather up my neck,
sharpen his razor on a strop,
and pass the sharp blade over my skin.
I was a sparrow gently held.
Years later, when I finally had sex,
the sparrow flew around the room, freed.

To the Young Man I Saw on the Street this Morning

I'm sick of writing poems to people like you.
Why don't you get out of my life?
All my friends are going to say,
that goddam faggot's writing about young men again,
impossible ones with Fra Angelico faces
and Caravaggio bodies
who smile divinely at him on the street (like you did),
whom he can't have because they're too good-looking,
too young, or straight,
and about whom he fantasizes at night.
Leave me alone!
I didn't ask you to materialize this morning,
your fine skin isn't my fault,
I didn't make those delicate, long lashes,
I didn't teach you to blush like that!
I'm going to start writing about responsible things,
scholarship, commitment, so please
go away,
let me be....

But wait.
There's one condition under which I'll write more poems
like this.
Come up, take my hand, kiss me, and take me with you
and I'll write you hundreds of poems like this. Thousands!

Sin

My parents taught me one of the worst things
you can do in life is blow into your straw
when your glass is empty.
They had no idea what Larry and I
were doing in my bedroom, and we had
the sense not to tell them.
I folded my towels, dusted my shelves,
displayed a pristine report card.
My parents were very proud
of a child they barely knew.

Crush on a Straight Man

It's totally useless,
like a spangle in a snowstorm,
a pimple one would like to get rid of,
a great poem wasted on the crowd.
It roots stubbornly in dense earth
and lolls its tongue out foolishly,
like a dog.

Spring

Damp cigarette butts, slick gum wrappers,
shreds of newspaper strewn on the café floor:
winter's detritus.
Pots of red and orange tulips on the counter,
raindrops beading on waxy leaves.
We made out for hours last night,
tongues savoring each other's every flavor.

Man Seen from Behind

I glance from my novel to see
a tall man in a maroon tee shirt
flexing his back at the tea bar counter,
his massive limbs and downy skin those of a proud elk,
his mane, a lion's tawny curls.
Is his voice stentorian?
Does he have a Norwegian accent?
Will the room explode if he laughs?

He shifts from one to the other of his sandaled feet,
which are a little big and awkward,
and softly orders tea,
sits down with his back to me.

I'm free to fantasize my favorite aquiline nose,
a fine bow of lips,
gold-flecked, green eyes—
to worship him, as though he were a statue
of Apollo or Mercury,
or a symbol of all that's beautiful in men.

I dream and dream,
even though I remind myself that, like me,
he has a beating heart,
worries, insecurities and to-do lists.
I dream, maybe because
I can't see his face.

I gaze at his solid shoulders,
his hairy neck and,
though I desire him, it's more than that.
He is perfect, his locks seem to me
like striations in stone,

his fingers narrow fish,
his shoulders elm branches,
his butt a rounded clamshell.
I dream that his face,
if I could view it,
would be like Mount Everest
emerging from clouds.

Maybe this is the man I've sought all my life.
What should I do?
Grab him? Kiss him?

I can't do anything
but sit here and imagine what his face looks like.
Maybe it's better that way.

Piedmont Avenue, Oakland Sonata

Drumbeat of rain leaves ebony roofs shining.
On the phone you're sad. What can I do
to infect you with my mood?
A sycamore's mottled limbs drip.
Cars and trucks continue their procession
down the Avenue,
unstopped by night or war,
each backfire, screech, horn a variation in a sonata
penned by the mysterious Piedmont Avenue Composer.
Until we meet in Berkeley for dinner
I'll sip Harmutty Assam and gaze.
The sun's bright enough to blind,
but in my tea, dances amber and citron.
Skittering sparrows skim the sidewalk,
kids laugh on their skateboards,
SUVs tumble down the street like harlequins.
See you at six.

JOHN SINGER SARGENT'S MALE NUDES

“Figure and Trees”

He’s limber as a larch,
his skin the color of bark,
muscles sturdy as branches,
gaze steady as a leaf.
He leans his right arm casually against the ground
and looks at you as directly
as the sun gazing at soil.
You’d like to embrace him,
but for the moment you
let him blossom in tans and browns.
You don’t want to spoil him with your touch.

“Figure on Beach”

His brown muscles flow like the water,
glowing sand, and rippling grasses
that carry him aloft,
a host hoisting a chalice
through golden day.

“Nude Study of Thomas E. McKeller”

He thrusts the fine gold china of his chest out proudly
and spreads his legs without reticence
to reveal his stubby brown cock.
The way he lifts and tilts his handsome head backward
is noble,
but it is his eyes, his liquid, speaking eyes
that make sex slave to his magnificent soul.

"Figure and Pool"

You want to reach out and touch his brown hillocks of flesh,
bite into his buttocks that resemble cinnamon toast,
turn him over to reveal his flowering secret.
But he's not alone.
He's there with bursting patches of soil,
quivering grasses, sloshing waves, bright coins of sunlight.
As he leans his lips forward to taste the water,
everything ripples and flashes into color,
and you love it as much as you love him.

"Mountain Stream"

This stream is crystal-pure as air rushing headlong
like blood in the veins under the firm, white skin
of the swimming boy near the curling ferns
and the naked rocks the water wets where the sun
bathes every pore with its liquid, golden, gurgling gift.

“Tommies Bathing” #1

Their midday nap permits these two shining men
to stretch their sun-starved limbs,
bend their knees with blissful abandon,
move their heads so close no one could say, no one,
whether they touch or not.

"Tommies Bathing" #2

You'd like to touch these radiant, light-infused men,
but they would kill you if you did.
One stretches head and shoulders back,
a nasturtium opening to the sun.
His whites and yellows are safe in the cool grasses,
which shield him from the others.
A second relaxes, lean, self-possessed.
A third, hair cropped, masculine,
naked back hard and curved,
enters the glinting water.
They are free to let it all hang out,
you are free to portray it from a distance,
savoring the liquid light on their skin,
but you can't lend smiles to their dangerous faces.

HEROES

Day and Night with Walt Whitman

Arise from the sleeping pavement, Walt,
large-limbed, generous-eyed, fleshy,
and sing with me a hymn of the city we love.
Of boisterous, crammed avenues awash with charging
cab and bus,
piers shifting with a score of mammoth liners,
neighborhoods teeming with Jew, Thai, Nicaraguan,
towers thrusting into air alive with light burst
and wind shimmy,
workmen straining sinew and tendon to fuse iron with iron
high among girders, beams, railings,
the policeman at the corner, proud, erect, manly,
his uniform gleaming blue as the waves of the Hudson,
the pinstriped businessman who confidently strides by
the worn beggar, both playing their parts in the pageant,
the ambulance that rips through the streets
carrying the mother about to give life,
the old man about to leave it—
the surge and seethe of it undiminished since your day.
Throw your arms around my shoulder,
let us mingle kiss and laugh
and stroll up Broadway together,
voices extolling fruit cart and deli,
boom box and pigeon.
Then spend one night in my bed—
two New York souls loving
the midnight city's quiet dark,
our words whispered into its ear.

Channeling Allen Ginsberg

Allen, buggering men in your pad on East 12th,
you soared in dharma visions above soggy mattresses
and crammed garbage pails heaped
on the midnight pavement,
pierced the phantom solidity of street lamps
and apartment blocks
with your keen gaze,
held up placards in Tompkins Square Park protesting war,
got New York high when it felt lonely.
Fellow Jew, Buddhist, gay, socialist, poet,
it's as though you laid the hard, glittering macadam
of the streets I love to tread.
You inspired me to relish the rubbery texture of dicks,
sit long hours peering into the void,
cry out against my country's bombs and jets.
Bearded, balding father, deviant muse,
may your howls ring out still in my words,
may your cock stiffen again when a man piques my fancy,
may your witty, sad eyes see me
through this endless web of streets.

Winging It with Kenneth Koch

Kenneth, your blossoms,
plump with nectar,
rained pulp down
on we who looked airwards from the streets.
Then you, a lark, ascended
to navigate cloud corridors,
sprinkling earthward notes
that relieved manholes of their covers,
and made dinner plates
slice through air like Frisbees.
Your breezes
lifted our hearts and our heads.
I try to sail, as you did,
above alleys and mews,
freshening city air
on wings,
with vowels.

A Little Night Music

for Arnold Schoenberg

Winter rain beats time to your
piano concerto's jagged leaps and runs,
my heart keeps pace with the jumpy rhythms
of the night and its moony fantasies.
My pen jots fragments of jazz notes
surging from zigzag movements of the dark,
turns toward dawn. I drowse,
my head abuzz with little strums and squeaks,
eeriness made close and comforting
by your hero's hand.

Russian Novels

Their authors are like exotic relatives I've never met. The tortured, disease-obsessed Dostoyevsky, an uncle who would have understood all my teenage angst. Turgenev, sympathetic cousin who would have supported my rebellion against my father. I would have liked to have thrown my arms around the neck of the wild-haired, white-bearded old Tolstoy and kissed him, crying, "Grandfather!"

Then, the characters. Blond, blue-eyed, self-effacing Sonya, niece of the Rostovs. Her impetuous, coal-eyed cousin Natasha. Shatov, such an overwhelmingly decent man I want to cry out when he's murdered. Alyosha Karamazov, my deep-down image of myself as naive, innocent, boy-like. Yet I threw away goodness, like Raskolnikov.

I am in their stories. Pacing with my musket in the snowy field, I too, like Pechorin, would have the pride to turn and fire at the man who insulted me. I've lain on my couch doing nothing for weeks, Oblomov-like. I'm insecure enough to imagine my nose cut off, living an independent life, à la Major Kovaliov. When I was married, the purity of my wife's and my love resembled Levin's and Kitty's.

Even the names—Nastasya Filipovna, Akaky Akakievich, Chichikov—fascinate. This expansive world: immense sky, clouds sweeping over broad steppes, streaming rivers, hamlets, willows, poplars. Indeed, my grandfather and grandmother hoed the loam near Minsk, killed and roasted chickens, sewed buttons on frock coats for the rich, poured their blood into me.

DAYS AND YEARS

Bosworth's

The shop was small, crammed with Pez
dispensers, Pet Rocks, Spillane novels.
While the Corner Store was modern,
spacious, owned by anti-Semites,
the Bosworth couple was friendly when
I bought school supplies or *Mad Magazine*
in that prosperous town where Ike's grin
assaulted us from a hundred windows.
I'd go to Bosworth's to talk with them
about their only son, dead in Korea,
whose smiling photo beamed down
from an upper shelf. I'd discuss my
poor attempts at trigonometry and
my awkward poems.
I'd hint at my parents' tyrannies
in words I barely understood myself.
It's been a long time but lessons
were learned, storms calmed, coats
outworn in this humble place.
Oh, Elmer and Betty, farewell.

Childhood Friend

I defended you from tease and taunt
at traipsing gait and flimsy wrist,
for though I played a mean hot corner
and could stalk the girls wolf-like,
on warm, moon-lit nights I was riding high
with you. Without saying how,
you knew to be top, me bottom.
The silk of your thick penis brought
a shiver that made me want to
play games, make up positions,
kiss in our secret garden where
hearts raced, created
a world in the hushed dark.

Fishing with My Father

It wasn't that often. Twice
at a lake in the Catskills,
once from a pier in New Rochelle.
Coppery sunfish, a mess of smelt,
one whiskered catfish we threw back.
He showed me how to hook
red wigglers, how to reel in.
His palm was soft
against my wrist, his breath
warm, so warm.

Harbor Island Beach

Instead of joining the expensive
Beach Point Yacht Club,
we went to public Harbor Island,
mixed with Italians, Poles, Blacks.
The sand was rough, the water
smelly, but a chance
to swim in the open sea.
There I ate fried hot dogs
split down the middle,
longingly read comic book ads
for Charles Atlas muscles,
wrote Clare Schulman love
letters before she changed her name
to Jaye and joined the fast crowd.
Distant now, but as real
as salt stinging my nostrils,
waves mixing with the smell of sewage,
sand burning my feet, as I
tiptoed through the shouting throng.

Provincetown in the 50's

The cheek-kissing sea spray drifting over
grass-studded lanes,
Portuguese fishing boats jiggling masts in the harbor,
gulls standing one-legged and staring on pier pilings,
long, narrow Commercial Street with its
lobster and crab restaurants,
crowds of tourists coming off the Boston boat to shop
for the afternoon,
stores with gray and white balsa wood gulls
and brass models of the Pilgrims' Monument,
chowder bars, tackle shops, clam and mussel stands,
gallery windows displaying watercolors of trawlers,
fishnets, anchors,
the large-bouldered breakwater racing
to the tip of the Cape,
New England natives, their sturdy white frame houses,
women in polka dot bikinis and pink sandals,
men, hand in hand, their pastel shirts, colognes,
willowy walks,
boisterous songs issuing from Hernando's Hideaway,
pointed looks, remarks, laughter—
Provincetown when I was a boy,
I who was alone, spoke to no one,
participated in none of this.

Cape Cod Fishing

We strode into the screaming surf at 9:00 P.M.
Jonah Rogers, my parent's friend, in
knee-high yellow boots and a black slicker,
me eight years old in sneakers, windbreaker.
I shivered as the undertow pulled
around my ankles. We cast our lines
into the spitting black waters higher
than our heads. Clouds rushed
across the sky, waves crashed
behind us, echoing my beating heart.
My line tugged, reeled in a skate,
flat as a board, two eyes on the top
of its head fixed on mine.
Mr. Rogers said, "Throw it back."
Around midnight the clouds cleared,
a full moon rose above the horizon.
Mr. Rogers put his hand on my shoulder.
It didn't matter we were empty-handed.

Secret

In Provincetown one summer
when I was fifteen
I pissed blood. The doctor
pronounced "urinary inflammation."
Two women with crew cuts
rented next door.
One day my father discovered
a rag soaked in blood by their fence.
He asked me if it was mine.
Knowing I shared a secret
with those women, I felt
I was lying—though I was not—
when I told him it was
theirs, not mine.

Camp Regis

I liked pussy willows, zinnias,
scarlet tanagers. While the other boys
punched and tackled, I made
my bed as neatly as a nurse.
I preferred to be alone, or joking
with my favorite counselor Stan
whose arms were lightly fuzzed with down.
Zorro, black gelding, was my friend—
I rode him out into the fields
where grasses grazed my calves.
If only I had liked myself more,
hadn't thought, I'm ugly and sad
and shy. Nothing to do
but wait it out.

Prep School

The student body was six hundred Jewish
boys. Don't let them tell you Jews aren't
good-looking: Jeremy's eyes were like
darting birds, Ken's nose a proof of God.
We wore black suits with tight pants, white
socks, narrow ties. Mr. Clinton was attracted
to the boys too but when he'd praise
Hal Poster's hair, I'd titter with the rest.
I'd drive to Yonkers with Jon and Andy
to bring the newspaper to the printer,
reveling in the nearness of their flesh.
I didn't touch a single boy. I wonder
what would have happened had I done
the unthinkable; would they have screamed
Faggot, faggot? I never found out.

Hypochondria

I was sure I had epilepsy
like my idol Dostoyevsky:
my arms and legs twitched,
I got dizzy in wet weather,
I suffered like him.
One day during a movie
a boy in front of me
convulsed, frothed
at the mouth, was carried out.
I was next, for sure.
But months passed
with no seizure.
I realized,
after a year of contemplation,
I was neither epileptic
nor Dostoyevsky.

Lozenges

I remember the black currant lozenges
I sucked while soaking in *Eine Kleine Nachtmusik*
in the college music center as snow
obscured the view and steam pipes
banged out their rougher music.
At eighteen, everything was new:
music, girls, boys. My mind was a
tabula rasa on which events traced
fragile patterns of fame, romance,
wisdom without any sense of how
to attain them. Our teacher was a man
with a wispy manner, a lisp,
and a gentle touch in playing Webern.
I admired and felt sorry for him.
Who was I to feel sorry for anyone?
I barely knew how to tie my shoes.
The lozenges were from some trendy
store, and gave me a bit of courage
to face the cold, our next exam,
and all I had yet to learn.

Edifice

We nerds used to dine together
in the college cafeteria,
then hit the books.
We were united
by low self-esteem.
One day I sat with
the cool kids at dinner,
was surprised they liked me.
I grew my hair long,
wore tie-dye shirts,
cold-shouldered my old friends.
Was I a cool kid now?
As I played at being cool,
I began to believe it.
Today, I carry around
a whole edifice of confidence
built on almost nothing.

Paris, 1966

I feel a pang recalling the lemon tea
that washed down a croissant in the café
across from the Luxembourg Gardens
when I was too young to have a sense
of tragedy. Everything bored its way
deep into memory: crones in black
collecting *sous* from the sitters in the Gardens,
visions of Rimbaud making the sky
tremble above those iron chairs,
exhaustion that plagued me after
every day of sightseeing.
No HIV had happened yet,
no breakdowns, no divorce,
but each sweet thing was tinged
with sadness, as though the world
was gently preparing me
for what would follow, like apricots
in brandy on a charcuterie shelf,
expanding, darkening, sweetening.

Mike Kortchmar

Mike Kortchmar has died at sixty-four,
broadcasts the alumni journal. He was tall
in high school, gray-eyed, sarcastic;
I stared, but never spoke to him.
His smile gathered girls around him.
He graduated before me, but we went
to the same college, where again
he was the center. Did he know
me? After he graduated, I glimpsed
him at the West End Bar on
Broadway, surrounded by hipsters,
that grin sharp as a blade.
Did he see me? Now the Reaper
has scythed that smile, that gray gaze.
Mike Kortchmar, I will
follow you again some day.

Gathering Rosebuds

for Ann

You were barely nineteen.
Who could have known I'd fall
so hard, find perfection in
your boy-like chuckle,
your way of running
like a drunken ostrich,
your apricot breasts?
We laughed so hard, naked
on the redwood cabin cot,
that I thought I'd found
the ultimate on my first try.
Couldn't you have waited a little
longer to deliver the chilling word?
You were young and only
wanted to have fun.
Couldn't you have taught me first
to take things less seriously?

The Dream

for Prudence

We sat on a garden bench drowned in wisteria.
My arm fit perfectly around your waist.
I drew you near,
felt the length of your glowing body,
smelled the fragrant oil of your hair.
When our heads came together,
our eyelashes merged,
we became the whole world.

But nothing had changed in the dream,
you were leaving.
It's been forty years,
you were still going,
nothing, nothing, nothing has changed.

Old Flame

for Prudence

Maybe you only left me
temporarily. Maybe you told me
you loved that French count
to pique my interest. Maybe
you married the Jewish doctor
to show me you could do
anything you wanted.
Maybe you were silent
forty years to make sure
I didn't forget you.
Now that I'm settled
and my life good
you've come back in it
as though you'd planned that
all along. The fact
we can't be together
is beside the point.
I'm not sure what you'll do next.

Love's Body

When I checked into the mental ward
I was prepared to be killed and
reborn into Love's Body,
my fantasy of naked lovemakers,
but I entered to please my parents.
I survived to smoke Winstons
at 2:00 A.M. with Lou and Meg
and the rotating nurses.
Jean and I joked about the bullet
she'd put through her head,
Anita held my hand like a long lost love,
Doug made friends with the openly gay guy
while I pursued and failed with Doug.
The food was poor, the "movie night"
silly, but Thorazine and Stelazine
put my head together and each day's
talk with George lent balance.
I miss the place.

My France

recedes farther and farther in my brain
with its roast boar, chanson crooners,
hamlets with names like
Bourg-en-Bresse and Jailly-les-Moulins.
It stirs at the back of my skull,
still alive. It was once flesh.
I lived it—chose plum tarts at Au Petit Duc,
traipsed down narrow, postered alleys,
recited Baudelaire in woods
with cuckoo birds talking.
Now it whispers memories in my ear.
Oh hexagon, how can you go on
without me, why don't you stretch out
a gloved hand and pull me languidly to you?
Why play a woman no longer in love?

Kibbutz Watermelons

Spitting seeds out into the sultry, heavy dark,
we sat, Esty, Ran, Jill and I, as Matti Caspi sang
rich, guttural words on the stereo inside.
No McDonald's here, no Comfort Inns,
just the love of Ran's parents Olek and Hannah,
brown fields of grass surrounding
the pear orchards where we worked, the dining room
piled up with tomatoes and cucumbers.
I never wanted to come here,
but now was intrigued by everything:
the sandals and shorts the men wore,
the sandy highway leading to Jerusalem,
Nazareth and Afula, the war memorial
at the center for those who had been lost.
What had I found? My center seemed nearby
but I never quite located it, yet thirty years later
still miss the scorching heat, the sabra rudeness,
walking down a street surrounded by Jews.

Star of David

The Star of David on the tombstone,
the bearded rabbi all in black,
the kaddish we recited for my father
all brought back that afternoon
my parents and I visited the Western Wall
and my dad wept, saying, “I’m going to give
that rabbi some shekels to say
a prayer for Pop.”

I’ve left instructions
that a rabbi say prayers over my grave
and hopefully some Jew or knowing person
will place a pebble on my headstone.

Mark

Eyes catching on Telegraph Avenue in Berkeley,
tongues and assholes locking that evening at my house,
I was cherry, you the master with the strong cock
who fucked me up and down three months.
We sailed through long days on your big mattress
in the middle of your floor in the Castro
with Crisco for lube, amyl nitrite for thrills.
Then you'd make baba ghanoush for dinner,
chaste sprouts, spinach, avocados, eggplant.
In the evenings we'd stroll Castro Street,
two among thousands pursuing a community of desire.
After I got sick, and rejected your bee pollen and garlic,
blaming my illness on you, we drifted apart—
then, once more only for a memorial fuck.

Survivor

I never liked peer pressure,
but all my friends were screwing
in parks, in alleys, in "tearooms"
where life was candy,
urging me to do the same.
I threw myself into it.
There seemed no end,
but one came—fever, sores, pain.
I blamed those friends,
so many of them now gone.

Who's Child-Eyed Now?

Wandering the streets at wit's end
after a year of illness and loss,
I glimpsed a red door ajar and behind it,
people dancing. I entered—why not?
There were managed groups of adults,
child-eyed, in capes, robes, ponchos,
twirling in circles and arabesques,
swinging their arms, shouting
as they beaded in sweat.
I grabbed two damp hands and linked up,
kicked my legs, swiveled my hips,
circled 'round, and gasped for breath,
laughing and laughing as we
sambaed, rumbaed, rocked.
I danced on, forgetting who they were
or who I was. Eventually I dropped
hands and found my way home.
When I think of shared humanity,
I remember that abandoned dancing.

Back from Canada

Sharp, smoky, drawling, raspy, clipped voices
melt in a stew:
I'm home.
Liberal news anchors, fine manners,
and immaculate gutters
are behind me.
I'm back with that shaved-headed man on his Harley
gunning down Piedmont Avenue,
kid who casually drops an empty Coke can on the sidewalk,
woman in the tea bar whose cell phone and laptop
click and clatter.

But when I mix in the supermarket line
with a Chinese man buying tofu and bok choy
and a guy from the Dominican
with whom I discuss Miggie Tejada,
a rich, dark music surges up.
Ours is a Picasso of jagged corners,
mismatched colors, and contorted postures.
We're thrown together in a salad
coated with vinegar, oil and pepper.
As I walk home, a man in his twenties
with soiled Princeton sweatshirt and tired eyes
asks for a dollar.
I give it to him, shake his hand,
go cook my meat and potatoes.

Hoops

One grad school day in Santa Cruz
Paul taught me
how to shoot hoops, defend.
About to quit,
we were challenged to a game
by two hairy, robust guys.
We were men,
what could we say?
We dribbled, ran, shot,
sweated, grunted,
guffawed, pushed off,
our perspiration mingled,
our breaths went in
and out each other,
eyes met,
arms grazed,
hands slapped,
thighs pumped,
until finally we were exhausted
and hugged, one by one,
dripping, burning,
ripping ourselves away
from the body of the game,
the single self we had become.

Springtime Return to Larchment

Maple trees sway in childhood's breeze.
Forsythia's scent mixes
with a mangy black dog's odor
and sassafras leaves soaked for tea.

Ducks and Canada geese in the lake,
an island in the middle we could only explore
when the water froze,
and "The Brook" that friends and I

dammed up so many times for kicks.
Nothing has changed:
the dazzling white dogwoods, the old Watson
house we thought was haunted,

the tree that split the sidewalk
(girls took one side, boys the other),
the steep hill where we sledded
our red American Flyers,

thrushes, chipmunks, turtles—
all here!
But some strange family's living
in Don Sackheim's house,

another one's invaded the Gerholds',
they've trucked in a whole load
of aliens to take over our town!
People are digging in our peony gardens,

parking SUVs in our driveways,
grinning to each other
across the privet hedges we planted!
I'm startled, incensed.

But then ... but then,
it isn't our town any more,
it isn't our youth any more,
all that belongs to someone else.

Awake

I sip some *Awake*, my first tea
after eight weeks of stomach pain,
procedures utilizing steel tubes
and probes, rubber gloves, urinals.
I'm healed, it seems, starting
a new life of lifting weights and
swimming to try to prolong my
mornings of French toast,
each slice golden-brown,
buttered, dripping with syrup.

Rising at 5:00 A.M.

for David

I exchange high fives with a Giants' fan
in Starbucks, joke with his green-eyed
girlfriend. A white-haired man crossing my path
salutes me as I let him go. Is that the sun
lifting its elbows above the gray table
of clouds? I exchange a word with the
bus driver taking me downtown, throw
a crumb of bagel to the junco
darting around my café table,
tell you I love you
when we talk on the cell.

"Fruit Perfection" Drink at *Jamba Juice*

for David

Peach, a fuzzed globe that dripped
juice down my chin as I took a break
from stickball on Briarcliff Lane in hot sun
that made the asphalt bubble and flow;
strawberry, a wild one I picked
along the pebbly road in Vermont under the
protective gaze of green hills and fields
of Queen Anne's lace in which my terrier
Kim dashed after gophers and chipmunks;
apple, the childhood of our race with its
Edenic pleasures of a world ripe with blossoms,
yet fallen in the end into poverty and war;
and mango, which I never knew as a
New York child, learned to like from you,
fellow California transplant, but lover of things
ripe, sweet and good—you peel it
for me, cut the pit out, and feed me
chunks with your hand: tart, tasty, juicy.

Streetlights

Morning sun shatters the silver ice of the horizon.
Streetlights seem elderly, having endured
all night with their steady light.
In *Jamba Juice* a “Fit ’n Fruitful”
freezes my dawn body. A jet draws
a crystal line across the sky.
Will I cross it?

Senior Diner

This is a place where we come to pass
the time that weighs heavy on our hands:
frail man in Kangol cap whose head shakes
as he orders toast and a poached egg, woman
with gray curls confiding something to her ancient,
squinting mother, balding guy in red
lumberman's shirt who chats up the waitress.
I itch all over, my leg hurts, I was in bed
by 8:00 last night. Now I'm here, it's midmorning,
and I don't know where I'm going.
Yet I enjoy each palsied word,
the hiss of water prepared for coffee,
the way the waitress leans over me
as she sets down my cereal and tea.

Tender Heart

I plunged a knife into my father's
huge, bald skull . . . well, in fantasy.
I was Dmitri Karamazov to his Ivan:
I thought the world a beating heart,
he, a pile of quarks and muons.
My mother's soulful arpeggios
on the piano battled his reason,
resounding through our house.
But, as I aged, yet kept my gay secret,
I came to mimic Dad's solid fortress.
I lived a world of numbers and ideas
and scorned her tender, racing fingers.

But now the secret's out, I'm soft—
my mother's son.

What Love Tells Me

is that some things go deeper than thought.
Quince blossoms, your lips on my cheek,
a line of song flowing on and on....
What can I wish for except what is,
since it includes your shoulders, your mild gaze?
I want to be like a melody that lingers
regardless of beginnings and endings.
To be like Mahler, who triumphed,
died young, left me this theme.

for David

Notes

"Old Baudelaire": Clare Cavanagh's translation of the Polish poet Adam Zagajewski's poem, "Old Marx (2)," appears on page 97 of her volume of Zagajewski translations, *Eternal Enemies* (New York: Farrar, Straus and Giroux, 2008).

John Singer Sargent's Male Nudes: The nineteenth-century society painter John Singer Sargent painted, secretly, many male nudes, especially of black men. See *John Singer Sargent: The Male Nudes* (New York: Universe Publishing, 1999). All the paintings my poems describe appear in this book.

"Russian Novels": Sonya, the Rostovs and Natasha are characters in *War and Peace*. Shatov is the hero of Dostoyevsky's *The Possessed*. Raskolnikov is, of course, the main character in Dostoyevsky's *Crime and Punishment*. Pechorin is the hero of Lermontov's *A Hero of Our Time*, Oblomov the protagonist of Goncharov's *Oblomov*. Major Kovaliov figures prominently in Gogol's story, "The Nose." Levin and Kitty are central figures in Tolstoy's *Anna Karenina*.

"My France": The French often refer to their country as "the hexagon" because it has that shape.

"Kibbutz Watermelons": Matti Caspi is an Israeli popular singer. A "sabra" is a person born in Israel. The word means "cactus," because native Israelis are thought of as tough and prickly on the outside, sweet within.

"Star of David": It is a Jewish custom for someone visiting a person's grave site to place a small stone or pebble on the headstone to indicate that they have been there.

"Back from Canada": Miguel "Miggie" Tejada is a current baseball player.

"'Fruit Perfection' Drink at *Jamba Juice*": Briarcliff Lane is in my hometown of Larchmont, New York.

"Senior Diner": "Kangol" caps are made in Australia.

"What Love Tells Me": This is an English translation of the name Gustav Mahler gave to the last movement of his Third Symphony: *Was mir die Liebe erzählt.*

About the Author

Marc Elihu Hofstadter was born in New York City in 1945. He received his B.A. degree from Swarthmore College in 1967, and his Ph.D. in Literature from the University of California at Santa Cruz in 1975. From 1977 to 1978 he was Fulbright Lecturer in American Literature at the Université d'Orléans, and in 1978 and 1979 he taught American literature at Tel Aviv University. In 1980 he obtained his M.L.S. degree from the University of California at Berkeley and, from 1982 to 2005, served as the librarian of the City of San Francisco's transit agency. He has published four other volumes of poetry, *House of Peace* (Mother's Hen Press), *Visions* (Scarlet Tanager Press), *Shark's Tooth* (Regent Press) and *Luck* (Scarlet Tanager Press) and his poems, translations, and essays have appeared in over sixty magazines and in the anthology of writings about tea entitled *Steeped*. Hofstadter is a member of one of the United States' leading intellectual families. His uncle Robert Hofstadter won the Nobel Prize in physics, his cousins Douglas and Richard Hofstadter were both awarded the Pulitzer Prize, his father Albert was an acclaimed philosopher, his mother Manya Huber a concert pianist, and his uncle Samuel Huber a noted painter. Hofstadter lives in Walnut Creek, California with his partner, the artist David Zurlin.